MW01094373

The Art of Self
Muscle Testing
For Health, Life and Enlightenment

Michael Hetherington
(L. Ac, Yoga Teacher)

www.michaelhetherington.com.au

info@michaelhetherington.com.au

Brisbane, Australia

Disclaimer

About the Author

Michael Hetherington is a qualified acupuncturist, health practitioner and yoga teacher from Australia. He has a keen interest in mind-body medicine, energetic anatomy, nutrition and herbs, yoga nidra and Buddhist style meditation. Inspired by the teachings of many, he has learnt that a light-hearted, joyful approach to life serves best.

Other Titles by the Author:

Chakra Balancing Made Simple and Easy

Meditation Made Simple

How to Do Restorative Yoga

Autumn Oriental Yoga

The Little Book of Yin

How to Learn Acupuncture

Simply Zen Quotes

Acknowledgements

I would like to thank Denise Robinson in Melbourne, Australia, for being my first teacher in Applied Kinesiology. I would also like to thank some of the pioneers in this field, Dr. Thie Goodhart, Dr. John Diamond, Dr. David Hawkins and Dr. Charles Krebs, whose ongoing work is truly inspiring. Special thanks go out to my partner, Angela Hammond, for her help with the photos and the endless hours of discussion on this topic.

Table Of Contents

Introduction

The purpose of this book is to help people to understand and apply the basic guidelines for accurate self muscle testing. It is a skill and tool that is incredibly valuable and I was inspired to write this book to help others have greater access to this skill. The more people who can successfully self muscle test, the better it is for all beings because muscle testing has the potential to rapidly enhance one's ability to "know thyself."

It takes some time and practice to get the hang of the self muscle testing technique, so don't be too disheartened or discouraged if it doesn't come easy to you initially. I hope, with the tips and tricks outlined in this book, that your ability to understand the technique and accurately self muscle test is greatly enhanced.

The term "muscle testing" sounds like it is used to simply test the muscles of the body, but in many therapeutic settings and in the context of this book, muscle testing also refers to being able to test more subtle levels of existence. Muscle testing has the capacity to work with very subtle energetic levels, namely the meridian pathways and the chakra's, to name just a few, therefore making it a very helpful tool to uncover deeper and more subtle levels of information. It depends largely on the individual tester and their level of understanding and experience with muscle testing as to how subtle and potentially how far they can go with it.

When first discovering the self muscle test, it will be natural to go through an experimental period where you do the muscle test on nearly everything you come into contact with. This experimental period will help you to fine tune your sensitivity and enhance your intuition, enabling you to feel the effect of these things on your energy field on a very subtle level. After your intuition and understanding of the technique has matured, the need to conduct muscle testing will probably tamper out, due to your deepened ability to sense the effect of things on your system. Until that time comes, be sure to explore and experiment with the self muscle testing methods so as to get established in the technique.

Benefit alone will come from muscle testing because this technique cannot be used for ill-will. If the intention of the testing comes from a place of greed, anger, envy, or any of these impure states, then the test will only give unclear, irregular and false feedback. If the testing is genuinely born out of curiosity, willingness, courage, detachment, and to sincerely understand and uncover the truth of things in the highest good, then the feedback of the test will be clear, consistent and affirming. Essentially, the self muscle testing technique helps us to identify those things that either support our life force or those things that do not.

The truth is that not all humans have the capacity to perform muscle testing accurately. There are certain prerequisites or conditions that are required to be in place before accurate and proper muscle testing can take place. These will be revealed and clarified in this book.

There is plenty of information on the internet regarding self muscle testing, energetic testing, applied kinesiology and some other self testing methods (which are all generally talking about the same thing), but few explain the ideal conditions required and the questioning skills needed in order to receive clear and concise feedback. Also, many of these resources explain the muscle testing procedure in the context of conducting it on another person, but few really go into the self muscle testing process in a thorough way.

What I have uncovered with my experience with self muscle testing is that you have to be 'switched on' before you can test. This is one of the main fundamentals required for accurate testing and this is what is not clearly explained in many of the resources online. Therefore, we will explore a variety of methods and processes to 'switch on' so that one can test effectively and accurately.

With the permission of the field of consciousness itself, I have embarked on this book to help clarify and empower others to establish accurate self muscle testing. May this book help to enable you to understand and apply accurate self muscle testing so that you can reveal the truths of your own body and mind as well as the truths of the universe.

Coming Into Contact With Muscle Testing

I first came into contact with muscle testing in 2006, when I began attending a health college in Brisbane, Australia, to study Remedial and Chinese massage. A rather eccentric looking teacher was offering extra tutorials and demonstrations on this strange new modality known as muscle testing to some of the students who were pursuing more advanced courses such as acupuncture and naturopathy. I was immediately drawn to it and I soon booked myself in for a consultation with the teacher.

After a few minutes with the teacher he began asking me odd questions and stating some basic truths that were relevant to me. For example, he asked me if I cooked my eggs till the yolk went hard and whether my legs tired easily after 20-30minutes walking. I answered both questions with a "yes", with the feeling that he already knew the answers but was seeking confirmation. He gave me some advice and nutritional supplements to take and after 15 minutes it was all over. I remember asking myself what had just happened. I couldn't understand what had occurred and so this experience only spurred on my interest in muscle testing.

Because I was already engaged in fulltime massage studies and working part time, I didn't pursue muscle testing for the next 2 years. In 2008, I moved to Melbourne, Australia, to find work and pursue other interests that Melbourne had to offer. I had completed my Diploma in Chinese acupressure massage but had gradually realized that massaging for more then 3-4 hours a day was very taxing on my body and overall energy levels. Deep down, I knew that massage wasn't quite what I was designed for and that there was something else within the healing world that would suit me better, but I wasn't aware of what it was or even where to look. So, I put it all on the back burner as I moved to Melbourne to set up a new life. Six months into my stay in Melbourne I discovered a "Touch for Health" course being held close to my house. "Touch for Health" is a healing system developed by one of the founders of applied kinesiology, Dr. Thie Goodhart. With my interest in muscle testing rekindled, I knew it was time I enrolled onto the course at the risk of losing my part time job.

A majority of the course was designed around learning how to effectively muscle test another person for therapeutic purposes. The "Touch for Health" course opened me up to a whole new level of treatment and a very practical way of working with energetics. Because of my previous studies in massage and Chinese medicine, I took to the course material easily and soon after the course I realized the possibilities that muscle testing offered were potentially infinite. Since then, I have been using muscle testing in all areas of my life. Initially it was very experimental, testing anything I could think of. I experimented with self-testing quite a lot and developed a way that suited me and gave me consistent and clear answers. After some time, it felt like I had developed such sensitivity to the muscle test that in many instances I could sense the response without needing to actually test.

In 2009, I went back to health college to upgrade my qualification in acupuncture and I also completed my yoga teacher training. I have since discovered ways of using muscle testing to enhance acupuncture treatments and I have used it to help me identify which paths of interest to pursue.

The greatest contribution that muscle testing offers us is the ability and clarity to make choices from the heart and not from the thinking mind. Muscle testing creates a bridge to our deeper energetics and through muscle testing we can more effectively read and connect with this deeper wisdom.

The Prerequisites for Accurate Self Muscle Testing

There are some fundamental prerequisites that are required for accurate muscle testing, both for testing on others and for testing on oneself. Not all humans have the capacity to do energetic testing; it's to do with each person's level of intention and level of consciousness. If you are drawn to this book and these teachings it is very likely that you have the capacity to do energetic testing. The level of consciousness simply refers to the state of "aliveness" and the general energy and intention that one carries around. If your general intention is to help others, to serve, to support others, to participate in life, to learn more about yourself and to realize who and what you really are, then this is a 'good' and uplifting state of energetic intention. On the other hand, if your general energy and intention is to take as much as you can get, to compete, defeat others, to be better than others, to prove others wrong, to drown oneself in sensual pleasures, to seek revenge and project anger and fear out into the world, then these types of intentions are more likely to be expressing a lower level of consciousness and are therefore non conducive to accurate energy testing.

The energy, intention and level of consciousness of people are expressed as the energy field they carry with them and radiate from their inner body. If their energy field is vibrant, flowing, inspiring, loving and caring than it's likely they have a higher level of consciousness. If they radiate hatred, anger, greed, judgment, shame, criticize others or carry a lot of guilt, then it's likely that their energy field will be heavy and expressing itself as a lower level of consciousness. To bring the level of consciousness and general energy field up to a healthy and beneficial state, simply surround oneself with natural beauty, nature, the arts, live a moral life, tame the senses, release guilt, give up revenge, work to serve others and purify the mind.

The following serve as a guide to help one come into this higher level of consciousness where more accurate energy testing can occur. They are:

1. A Moral Life

This does not refer to any particular religion or dogma, for it is a universal truth applicable to all humans. A moral life means that one is in the energy field of intention that is here to support life and not to destroy it. The ability to accurately muscle test depends a lot on the energy field of the tester. If the tester has a level of consciousness where the mind is full of greed, fear, anger, lust, guilt and shame, just to name a few, the energy field of this person is likely to be too unstable, fragmented, unbalanced and volatile to give accurate results when testing. The consciousness and state of the mind of the tester needs to be fairly devoid of those negativities and instead needs to harbor more supportive, nurturing, caring, selfless, giving, loving and integrous qualities within their energy field for them to have a greater chance of receiving accurate testing results. These higher states of mind and consciousness come from the practice and cultivation of a moral life.

The general ones that are listed here are from the Buddhist tradition, known as the 5 precepts, but these guiding precepts can be found in any tradition and were spoken of by every saint who has come to Earth in their own way. They are:
No killing
No stealing
No lying
No sexual misconduct

No intoxicants

- *No killing.* The reason for not killing is because the quality of the mind needs to harbor intentions of ill will and harm before it can kill another. Harboring these intentions within causes internal suffering and disturbs the balance of the mind. Many may ask and question, "What about eating meat? Do I have to become a vegetarian?" In the case of eating for food to support one's life energy, if one kills and eats an animal to support the body for continuing one's life and there is a sense of gratitude towards the animal that has been killed then, because of the intention and the gratitude, it would be generally be ok to eat meat.

On the other hand, if one has plenty of food available without the need to kill an animal for eating, then what is the intention for killing? If it is to simply fulfill one's desire for meat, or to prove or generate pride and ego from killing another being than this intention does not support life and therefore does not develop a balanced and pure mind.

- *No stealing.* This one is fairly straightforward. For anyone to steal they must develop the desire of greed in their minds in order to steal. Therefore this is not an act that supports life force.

- *No lying.* Again, this one is fairly straightforward and obvious. When you lie you are deceiving others. And why deceive others? To get something you desire. The mind becomes unbalanced and one has to continue to lie to keep the original lie in tact, adding more stress and anxiety to oneself. Therefore, it is advised not to lie in order to cultivate a more balanced mind that is suitable for accurate muscle testing and meditation.

- *No sexual misconduct.* No sexual misconduct refers to inappropriate sexual relations with another, like having sexual relations with your friend's wife, or another family member or a child etc. Such behavior develops and cultivates desire, lust and greed in one's mind. Having these inappropriate sexual relations tends to add a lot of extra stress, anxiety and drama to one's life. Best to avoid anything that disturbs the peace of your mind and that of the minds of others.

- *No intoxicants.* The main reason for this one is that if one becomes intoxicated than one is more likely to break the previous precepts, to lie, to kill, to steal etc. It also disturbs the clarity of the mind and the ability to meditate. Personally, I still drink alcohol and other things on rare occasions and sometimes find them quite helpful to relax, to socialize and connect with others and even gain some great insight into the mind and myself. When I am under the influence of these substances though, I still focus on keeping my other precepts in tact and avoid becoming intoxicated to the point where I lose the capacity to return to my center.

If you do take intoxicants, ask yourself if it is done out of habit, craving or desire. If you take the substance out of habit, attachment, greed or to run away from things, than this is a sign that the mind is unstable and this is a harmful condition. For a balanced state of mind, make sure you always take yourself off whatever substance it is for some time to break all mental and behavioral habits before taking it again. And never attempt to muscle test, for someone else or for self testing, if under the influence of intoxicants.

2. To Be "Switched On"

Switching on simply refers to the state experienced when your *energetic systems are at full function* and are therefore able to be tested. This is not a new concept or discovery. Dr. Goodheart incorporated the process of "switching on" into the touch for health system from its earliest days. The switching on process is vitally important for any applied kinesiology or for any energy testing to occur.

Some books and muscle testing systems sometimes call it a state of "physiological reversal". This is not an accurate naming for the condition because this type of dysfunction is not solely on the physiological level; it is expressed through the energetics of the body more so than just the psychological level. Having your energetic system at full function means that the energy flowing through the meridians is flowing smoothly, without obstruction or deficiency. This energy flowing through the meridians supports and fuels the nervous system that then plugs into the muscles. So if all is working at full function, we are able to test the muscles, which give us a response from the nervous system, the meridian system and potentially more subtle fields or dimensions of the body and mind. It's like if you go to play an instrument but it hasn't been cleaned, polished or tuned for some time. If you go to play the instrument in its unclean and un-tuned state, it can only produce an off-key, distorted vibration that probably doesn't sound too good. No matter how hard you try, the instrument won't correct the distorted vibration of sound that is produced. Similarly, with our energetic system (also a state of vibrations) and our physical structure, if you do not tune up or clean your energetic system when you go to play it, it will only deliver unclear, off key, distorted vibrations and therefore will only give unclear results when muscle testing. You need to 'switch on' by tuning up and cleaning the energetic system so it's ready for testing.

Before we go into explaining how to switch on, it's important to explore and explain what it feels like to be 'switched off'. Switched off means that at least one of your meridians (energy circuits travelling within and around your body) is impaired and not flowing well. Your instrument is out of tune. It often feels like your head is foggy and unclear and your concentration is not so good. The body's posture may be slumped and the digestion or belly often doesn't feel very good. If you have the sensitivity of awareness, you can feel some parts of your body don't feel very energized while other parts feel over energized.

I find with computers that the back of the body loses its energy because it slumps into a chair and the muscles become inactive because they aren't being used to hold the body up. This weakens the flow of the energy in the back of the body. At the front of the body, the shoulders and abdominals start to curl over, becoming tight and therefore disturbing the flow up the front of the body. This is a classic case of switching off. Sitting for too long at a computer desk, in a poorly designed chair and driving in a car will all have this effect. Generally, the human body isn't designed to sit for more than 4hrs a day, especially in the same chair. You know that feeling if you have a nap in the middle of the day and then you get up and try to function normally but you feel really dreamy, or foggy, and you just can't shake it—that's the feeling of being switched off. We often go for caffeine or some stimulant to feel that switched on feeling and, yes, caffeine does help us to do that for a short time as it draws energy from the kidney stores and uses it to pump through the whole system potentially overriding obstructions or deficiencies, though it's not the healthiest way to go about it. If we continue to use things like coffee, energy drinks and other stimulants to obtain energy, we are actually taxing our internal energy stores that are meant to support us in our older years. If we burn these stores up early in our lives, we will age very quickly and probably shorten our life span by at least a few years. So, how to switch on without having 3 cups of coffee in the morning?

How to "Switch On"

In this chapter, I explore the different methods I have uncovered that can help us to switch the energetic system on for more accurate muscle testing. Before you attempt any muscle testing on yourself, be sure to 'check yourself' and make sure you are switched on beforehand. If you are not 'switched on' results will be foggy, unclear and confusing.

To 'check yourself' means to observe how you feel and observe the state of your mind. Does my body feel alive, balanced and 'switched on'? Does my mind feel calm, clear and alert? Well, if so, you are likely to be 'switched on' and will receive clear and accurate results with the muscle testing—if not, you will need to do some of the following switching on techniques.

Even if you initially feel 'switched on,' you still need to keep a tab on your posture, breath, emotional state and your state of your mind—keep 'checking yourself' every now and then to make sure that you're still switched on. When you let your posture lose its integrity, or you feel that emotions have taken you over, or your mind becomes foggy and unclear, this means you have more than likely 'switched off'. So you will need to go through again and switch on—check yourself, and then you can return to any testing.

Our ability to hold the 'switch on' energetic state is different for everyone and has a variety of factors that influence it. Often we can simply 'switch on' by doing a number of the techniques listed in this chapter. But, if our general, every day energetic state is usually in the state of being switched off, than we will return to that state pretty soon after we have done some of the techniques to switch ourselves on for testing. It is usually anywhere between 2-10 minutes before the old energy pattern will re-establish itself.

Now, for those people out there who are quite active, exercise regularly, have good posture, good diet, live a moral life with an open mind and have the ability to concentrate easily, these people will generally be more 'switched on' in daily life than switched off. Those who do no exercise, sit in chairs all day, eat poorly, have poor posture, live a harmful, greedy and immoral life, and have no ability to concentrate are more than likely to be in a 'switched off' state most of the time. One of the goals for the latter person would be to bring more things into their life that switch them on like exercise, better food choices, a moral life and generating a better posture, to name a few. Factors such as which TV shows and movies you watch, books you read and music you listen to also influence your energetic system, which can either cause your system stress or uplift it. The general rule of thumb is, anything that glorifies violence, greed, stealing or lust, or causes harm (adds stress and anxiety) to other beings, is harmful to your energy field and also those around you will act to switch your system off to a state where you can't perform muscle testing. Anything that supports life, that is loving, integrous and does not intentionally harm other beings will assist your life force and will act to switch it on and make it stronger and more powerful (power in a positive, influential and spiritual sense as apposed to power in an egocentric, greedy sense).

Therefore, to raise the overall health of body, mind and heart and all beings, it is recommended to surround yourself only with those things that support life force (this is especially so for those who are ill or weak). The more you do this and the longer you do it for, the stronger your energy field will become and you will be more often in a 'switched on' state, meaning that your body is in a state of energetic healing and you can muscle test at almost any time without doubt or hesitation and receive very clear answers.

There are a few exceptions to the general rule of "surround yourself with only beneficial, healthy, positive things and avoid all those things that may have a negative effect on your energy field." I have seen many people go into a type of hysteria regarding this as they create so much anxiety and stress around trying to constantly avoid certain environments, foods or things that may be harmful. The truth is that sometimes these things are unavoidable because we cannot control our environment 100% of the time, so sometimes we will be faced with it. So when we are, don't loose the balance of your mind by creating stress and anxiety around it, just accept it for now and when it changes just move on. If you loose the balance of the mind and become very anxious about this, often this will cause more stress to your system than the actual object itself. Therefore, in such a case, best to just accept it and keep the mind calm and relaxed.

Another exception is that when some beings reach a highly evolved state of consciousness they tend to transcend all the negative (and positive) effects of the environment they are in because it seems that the effects of the external world have lost their power over them. For such beings, eating a McDonalds Big Mac burger will probably have no ill effect on them.

To help give you a better understanding of this, I have created a table below. One column displays those things that harm life force and the other one displays those things that support life force. To increase one's health on all levels and increase our capacity to receive accurate self-muscle testing, bring at least 80% of those things that support life into our daily life and reduce or avoid those things that harm life force. This can be confronting for many people—if so, you don't have to agree with it but I ask that you just sit with it for some time and let the truth of it reveal itself.

Supports Life Energy	Harms Life Energy
General Attitudes Lets work together. How can I help? We are all different and there is no better than… Somehow I created this situation and I will take steps to change it. There must be a better solution. Let's try again. Appreciation, gratitude. Calm, patient.	General Attitudes I win, you lose. I want… I deserve… I am better than… Us vs. Them. They did this to me. Why me? Poor me. I give up. I can't be bothered. I could never do that. Winging, complaining. Impatient, intolerant, fearful, greedy.
Relationships Supportive, honest, caring, good communication, generous, loving, giving, thoughtful, considerate, appreciative, inspiring.	Relationships Demanding, manipulative, exploitative, disempowering, controlling, violent, abusive, dishonest.
Music Acoustic, classical, folk, ambient, most easy listening, jazz, world music, happy go lucky.	Music Rap, heavy metal, death metal, R'n'B, most pop music, most club dance music, some electronic.
Films Most drama, nature, some doco's, musical, comedy, some fantasy, some kids.	Films Horror, most action, revenge plots, anything that glorifies crime.

TV Shows	TV Shows
Inspiring, some comedy, educational, some sports, cooking without competition.	Sitcoms, reality TV, commercial TV, news.
Sports	Sports
Soccer, golf, most martial arts, gym, walking, running, Olympics.	Boxing, fighting, animal fighting, hunting.
	Foods
Foods	Packaged and processed foods, sugars, alcohol.
Home cooked meals, fruits, vegetables, water, tea.	
	Self Care / Hygiene
Self Care / Hygiene	Chemical deodorants and perfumes, chemical toothpastes, chemical shampoos, hair spray, home and car deodorizers.
Natural soaps, essential oils, organic and natural shampoos, generally least amount of chemicals in products, tea tree, eucalyptus.	
	Other
Other	Addictions—gambling, drugs, alcohol, sex, power, drama, talking, food, shopping, video games.
Able to change and adapt without losing the balance of their mind. Lets go of trying to control others and life.	

Ok, so let's get into some specific techniques to 'switch on' so we can perform more accurate muscle testing.

Switching On for Testing

Here is a list of various techniques that help to switch on our energetic systems. Feel free to experiment with them and, when you find one, or more, that suit you, practice them often. After some time working with these techniques you will come to know what works for you and when you are in a switched on state and when you are switched off.

1. Clinical Kinesiology Method

In the practice of "touch for health" and other applied kinesiology systems, they teach you to rub acupuncture point Kidney 27, place the palm over the belly area, they also rub points at the base of the skull, rub either side of the spine at the upper back and at the lower back and sweep the hands up the front of the body like a zip to encourage the energy up the central meridian to the brain. Most kinesiologists tend to shortcut their own process in regards to this.

So for those who are not trained in these systems, simply try:

1. Rubbing Kidney 27 acupuncture point.
The Kidney 27 points are one of the most powerful points on the body. Rubbing them throughout the day can increase overall energy flow and help to clear the mind.

K27 is located in the hollow depression just under the collarbones, just next to the breastbone.

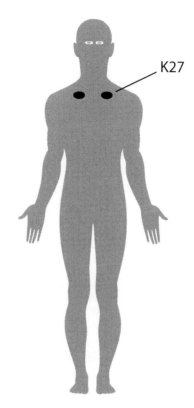

K27

2. Rubbing your lower belly.

3. Rubbing at the base of the skull.

4. Rubbing either side of your spine at the upper back and lower back.

5. Sweeping a hand up the front of the body (hand just away from physical body) to encourage energy up the central meridian to the brain.

6. Then have a sip of water and 'check yourself.'

This process is great if you are doing the testing on somebody else because you can easily get to these points over their body. But, in the case of self testing, many points of the body are simply not accessible with the hands and arms so, while this method is great when working with another person, this isn't the most practical method to switch on for self testing.

2. Yoga, The Feldenkrais Method or Any Neuro-Muscular Activation

If a yoga class or exercise class or workout is balanced, meaning all the main muscle groups are activated and stimulated, it will likely switch your energetic system on for some time. If the yoga class or exercise does not provide a balanced workout, and therefore only switches on a few muscle groups and not others, then sometimes this can leave you switched off. To give you an idea of what I'm talking about, the main areas that need to be activated are:

1. Front of the body (abs, pecs, anterior deltoid, thighs)

2. Back of the body (buttocks, lower back, upper back, back of shoulders)

3. Main muscles in the legs (thighs, hamstrings, calves)

4. Main muscles in the arms (deltoids, biceps, forearms)

The most important of these is the first two. The front of the body and the back of the body both need to be switched on as these are the main channels that govern the flow of energy up the front of the body (Ren channel) and also up the back of the body (Du channel). We will discuss these channels in further detail in the following pages.

The easiest way to activate the "Ren" and "Du" channels of the body is to do some form of strengthening the shoulder blades on the back of the body and the chest muscles on the front of the body.

Here is a list of exercises that I have found that effectively switch on the muscles associated with the Ren and Du energy channels.

Du (Back) Channel Activation

Chair Dips
Main benefit – Activates the upper back and arm muscles

1. Find a stable chair or a big block that can easily support your weight.
2. Place you hands on the chair or block, finger pointing forwards and step your feet out so that when you dip down your knee will be at around a 90 degree angle.
3. When your ready dip yourself up and down to activate the upper back and the arms. Be sure not to dip down too far putting excess strain on your joints. Dipping just a short distance is enough to activate the right muscle group.
2. Do at least 10 dips to get the upper back fully activated.

Locust Pose
Main benefit – Strengthens the back of the body

1. Lie on your belly in the middle of your mat.
2. Bring the arms down the side of the body, palms facing up. Feet hip width apart. Looking forward, resting the head on the chin.
3. On an inhale start to raise the upper body off the floor. Raise the arms and hands off the floor. Try to get the arms parallel with the floor.
4. Then start to raise the legs off the floor. Try to keep your legs straight.
5. Look diagonally down towards the floor to keep the neck inline with the spine.
6. Now gently squeeze the hands towards each other so you activate the muscles around the shoulder blades.
8. Keep the breath moving. Hold fro 3-4 breathes and then slowly release and relax back onto your mat.
9. Have a little rest for a few moments and do it at least 1 more time.

Ren (front) Channel Activation

Down Facing Dog
Main benefit – Strengthens arms, shoulders and opens back of legs

1. Come onto all fours with hands underneath the shoulders and knees under the hips. Spread your fingers wide.
2. Tuck the toes under, start to extend the arms and start bringing the knees off the floor.
3. Come to extend the arms, and start to work the kegs straight. Try to bring the weight back into your legs and not so much into your arms.
4. Look to the floor just under your belly button.

Pushups (variation – knees on the floor)
Main Benefit – Activates and strengthens the chest and abdominals

1. Come onto your hands, spread the fingers wide and squeeze the floor slightly with your hands. Toes tucked under. Try to get your body into a straight line.
2. With control, slowly lower yourself towards the floor and on the exhale push yourself back up to the original position.
If you have trouble with the traditional pushup, you can always place your knees on the floor and do it that way.
3. Aim for around 8-10 pushups to fully activate the muscles on the front of the chest.

Everybody is different and has a different capacity to hold their energetic structure in a switched on or switched off mode. Generally speaking, if you do a yoga class or a balanced exercise class/session in the morning then it will likely leave you switched on for most of the day. If you don't do class or an activation process in the morning you will probably be switched off for most of the day. This is why it is usually stated that exercise in the morning gives more benefit than that done in the evening. Many people go for coffee first thing in the morning rather than exercise because it does give that feeling of being 'switched on'. Though coffee drains the internal energy over time and can leave you feeling very flat or fatigued whereas exercise generally tops up the internal energies, providing a sustained and invigorated energy supply.

I know in the case of yoga that stronger yoga is better suited to the morning as energy is rising and the softer, more nurturing practices are better suited to the evening because the energy is being drawn downwards and is more internal.

3. Running the Meridians

This technique is simply using your hands to run the meridians (also known as flushing the meridians) in the right direction, stimulating the system towards a "switched on" and highly functional state.

You can, of course, flush all the 12-14 meridians on the body but this takes a lot of time and knowledge in understanding where they flow and in which direction they travel.

The easiest and quickest way to do this is to focus on the two main ones—the Ren channel that runs up the midline of the body and the Du Channel that runs up the back of the body.

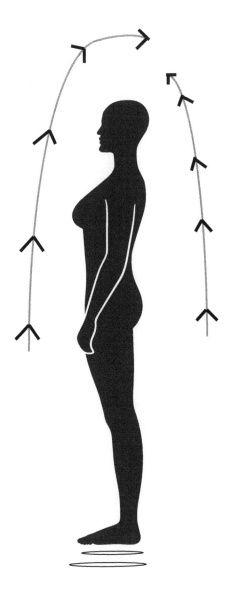

The front channel is known as the *Ren* channel and it travels up the midline of the body from the base of the torso to the very top of the head. The back channel is known as the *Du* channel and it travels up the spine from the base of the torso to the top of the head. These two channels connect up and continuously feed and nourish each other to support overall life force.

You can "run the meridians" on yourself or on somebody else. When you do it on yourself you can only really access the front channel (Ren channel) and that's ok. When doing it on somebody else you can do both, which adds a bit more energy and power to it but it's not absolutely necessary. I've found it easier to do on others so this is a good one to do with friends and loved ones.

Doing it on yourself:

1. Check yourself that you feel clear and your intention is simply to support life energy.

2. If sitting, sit up with straight spine, if standing, stand balanced on both feet, knees slightly bent, if lying, make sure you're lying flat and comfortably. A pillow is ok but not a really big one that cricks the neck.

3. Place one of your hands just away from your body, down at the base of your torso near your groin. Palm is relaxed and facing upwards, as if you are holding a bowl.

4. Then slowly start to draw the hand up the front midline of your body, up to the very top of your head, and let it curl over the top of your head.

5. Repeat by bringing the hand back down to the groin, place the hand into the position, like holding a bowl, and sweep it up the front of the body again.

6. Repeat about 3-5 times slowly; if your arm tires, rest it for a moment.

7. Now, repeat the action but when you get to the top, turn the palm slightly downwards and draw it down to the groin. So now you will be going up and down the front of the body.

8. Repeat going up and down 3-5 times. If the arms get tired, rest them.

9. To finish, make sure you finish with the hand going upwards.

10. When you're ready, rest your arm. How do you feel now?

Here are some photos.

Doing it on somebody else:

1. If they are sitting, have them sit with a straight spine on the edge of the seat so you have access to their back. If they are standing, advise them to stand relaxed and balanced on both feet. If they are lying down, have them lay on a flat comfortable surface (small pillow is ok). If they are lying down you won't be able to access their back but that's ok, just focus everything on the front channel.

2. Begin by placing one of your hands with the palm up, just away from their body at the base of the torso, near the groin. Then slowly and gently begin to sweep that palm up the midline of the body all the way to the top of the head. It helps to let the hand curl over the top of the head towards the back of the head to completely flush the meridian.

3. Continue with Step 2 at least 3 or 4 times.

4. Then try going both ways starting from the base of the torso upwards and then, from the top of the head, turn the palm downwards and flush the meridian downwards as well. Repeat up and down motion 3-4 times.

5. To finish, always finish with a flush or two going upwards.

6. If you have access to the back of the body, repeat the same steps as on the front of the body, first flushing upwards 3-4 times then flushing both ways 3-4 times and finish by flushing upwards one or two times.

4. Meditation

Meditation is something else that, if practiced in the morning, will likely switch you on for most of the day. Again, a lot depends on the person and the lifestyle they are engaged in as to how long and to what effect that person is able to remain in a 'switched on' state.

Meditation cultivates concentration, balances, purifies the mind and uplifts the life force. It really is incredible, and the effects are multi-dimensional. I advise people to work towards being able to sit in silence, with a balanced posture, for at least 5 -10 minutes. It will take at least this amount of time before the energetic system will start reorganizing itself towards a more balanced state. The first 10 minutes is generally the hardest as the mind tends to really resist it, but if you just continue to sit and relinquish the mind's thoughts and images for those 10 minutes, it tends to quieten down and loose its dominance. The longer you can sit, the better, and the longer the energetic balance will likely hold. Place your attention on the entry point of the nostrils and watch the breath as it moves in and moves out as this provides you with an anchor. Sitting for 20 minutes upwards is usually enough to fully balance out the brain and energetic structure and, therefore, 20 minutes is the amount of time most recommended. If you are new to it, then just start at 5, then 10, then 15, then 20, building up slowly over time.

There are many meditation techniques out there; many promise great and wondrous things, but don't get too caught up in all that. Meditation is not about chasing wonderful experiences; it's about getting real. Simply sitting in silence, with yourself, watching your breath, observing the mind's behavior and just accepting whatever arises is the art of it. Continuously relinquish thoughts, images and fantasies as they arise. Simply focusing on watching your breath come in through the nostrils and out through the nostrils is really enough. That's it! Let nature do the rest.

There are, of course, more advanced techniques out there, Vipassana or Insight meditation are the ones I highly recommend, but before embarking on these, especially if you have had no experience with meditation as yet, just get established at watching your breath and relinquishing the mind as thoughts and images arise. Allow space to be cultivated within. Sit for at least 5-20 minutes. This is all you need for now—benefits will come of their own accord.

5. Self Chi Bath & Massaging the Ears

Rub your hands together until they are warm and then start gently brushing your hands over your face, head and neck. Then again rub your hands together to create some warmth and then run them over your chest, belly and lower back. Then again, run the hands together to create warmth and then run them over the outside of the legs, up the insides of the legs, down the arms and up the inside of the arms. If you do this a few times, it will leave you feeling very relaxed yet very invigorated. This process re-establishes the flow of the meridians and therefore will switch you on for some time.

Massaging the ears is even simpler; simply start rubbing and massaging your ears at the same time. You can really get into them, pulling and rubbing them. Get into the harder parts of the ears and get the sense of uncurling the ears also. You want them to feel a bit hot. If you do this for at least 1 minute, you will surely feel very different and very likely to be switched on—just be sure to check your posture also.

This works because, in Chinese medicine, the ears replicate the whole body, especially the kidneys which are two of the most important organs as they harbor the source of all the energies. The effect is also powerful because the ears are very close to the brain and therefore the brain and nervous system are very stimulated when working with the ears. It is recommended to massage the ears at least once a day for good health.

1. Pulling down on the lobes   2. Pulling back and unfurling the ears

3. Pulling up on the ears

6. Natural Objects and Sacred Geometry

Looking at objects can also have a direct affect on your energy flow and meridians. Staring at or simply observing a tree in nature has a positive effect on our energy field. It's when we add stories and begin to analyze the tree with the mind that we begin to lose its full effect because we lose the energetic presence and connection with the natural object. If we feed these analytical thoughts with energy they will soon turn into stories that will go on massive tangents. Our emotions will soon get involved and it will likely create a stressful response on our energetic system. To look at nature without adding stories or thoughts of analysis to it keeps you present and will support the life force of both oneself and the natural object that is being witnessed.

I realized that sacred geometry would play a part here also and discovered that the flower of life was one expression that could do this.

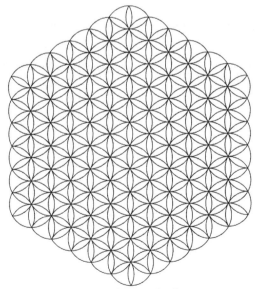

Image: Flower of Life

This phenomenon is, of course, not limited to just the flower of life. Most structures that are bilateral, symmetrical in design, will have a balancing effect on the nervous system and potentially put you into a 'switched on' mode. Though, from my testing, you need to hold the image as your point of concentration for at least 10 minutes to put you in a switched on state to do accurate muscle testing, which is quite a long time for most of us. The other methods here can switch you on a lot quicker. Regardless of how long it takes, having sacred geometry patterns around your house and workspace will definitely contribute to a more balanced energy and nervous system that will affect all beings that enter that space.

Shri Yantra – An image of universal balance used in the yoga's.

Balancing images don't have to be as complicated and intricate as those used in many artistic expressions of sacred geometry. Balanced images can also be very simple.

Let's have a look at some other simplified patterns.
These patterns are balanced (bilateral), meaning that these images don't stress out the neurological system when looking at them. You can muscle test these up later by simply gazing at them and self muscle testing.

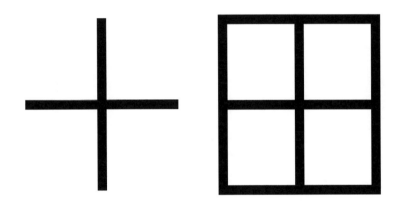

Now let's have a look at unbalanced patterns.

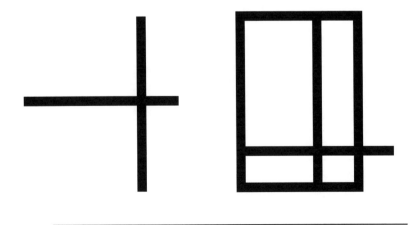

Now, how do they make you feel? Later on, come back to these images and muscle test them while gazing at them. What happens?

These images provide you with an example of how patterns and images can directly affect your life energy through the nervous system. It is best to surround yourself with images that are bilaterally balanced, therefore naturally supporting life force and balancing the nervous system.

Let's look at another example, a triangle.

Now the triangle pointing downwards...

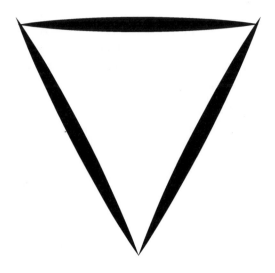

What do you feel when you gaze at each one?
The triangle pointing upwards lifts energy upwards whereas the triangle facing downward pulls energy down. Try muscle testing it as you look at each one. You want to avoid the energy being drawn downwards; therefore it's not a good idea to have an upside down triangle as a logo or on any material in your house or related to your business.

6. Classical Music

Because of the highly sophisticated nature of classical music, it holds a very supportive energy field that balances out the nervous system quite quickly. If you were to listen to classical music, without other distractions, it would begin to switch us on after about 2 minutes. It depends a lot on the individual and the current state of their energy field before listening to the classical music as to how long they would need to listen to it to become fully switched on. You will most likely have to experiment with it for yourself to get the sense of it. Doing some yoga or some exercise while listening to classical music will likely switch you on much faster than if you remained in a sitting, passive state.

I've found it to be very supportive when I play classical music in a clinical setting as it really elevates the healing power of the space and the people exposed to the music. I find it also helps me when I'm writing or studying. I tend to avoid the really dramatic and full on sounds of classical music and prefer the gentle and more relaxing expressions of it.

7. Mudra (Hand Positions)

Placing your hands into a certain position simply encourages a certain energy flow in your meridian system. It's actually very powerful stuff; the trick with any mudras is that you really need to hold the hands in position for at least 2 minutes to start gaining the full benefits and to give the body a chance to re-establish the energetic flow. Simply taking 2 minutes to stop running around, sit down and settle the hands into a mudra, really calms the mind into a much more balanced and peaceful state.

Anytime I feel tired, exhausted or flustered, I know it's because, somewhere along the line, I've let my energy flow out and have become fragmented. I know that I have not taken enough time out to re-establish my energy flow. Sitting in a chair or in meditation with the fingers interlaced for 2 -5 minutes can make a world of difference. Crossing the fingers helps the left and right sides of the brain integrate and stabilize.

Another suggestion is to just sit comfortably, interlace your fingers and rest them on your lap. Watch your breathing, relax the body and just stay there for at least 2 minutes. Relinquish any thoughts and emotions as they arise, come back to watching your breath and sensing your body. You can close your eyes or keep them open, but I find closing the eyes helps calm everything down a lot quicker.

I find my hands get really warm and my arms start buzzing, my mind becomes very calm, my breath stabilizes and everything feels settled. Then I know I'm in a good space where I can then move on to my next task which may involve muscle testing. This is a good thing to do between seeing clients. Just give yourself 2 minutes to sit, interlace your hands, rest and breathe. Try it out.

Here are some other hand positions that I have found that will switch you on after holding them for at least 2 minutes.

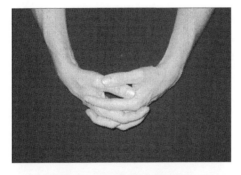

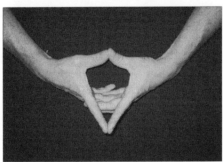

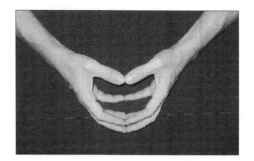

Self Muscle Testing

Ok, so we have covered how to create an environment that supports life force and we have also covered how to "switch on" so that we will be in a heightened state to conduct accurate self muscle testing. So, now it's time to go into how to do the actual self muscle test.

For the main method described in this book we are primarily using and isolating a small group of muscles in the hand for the testing. The muscles are called opponens pollicis, abductor pollicis brevis and adductor pollicis.

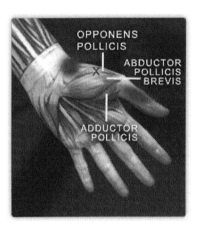

This muscle is found on the inside of the palm and acts to flex the thumb towards the little finger. It originates on the tubercle of the trapezium bone and the flexor retinaculum and inserts onto the anterior and lateral surfaces of the shaft of the first metacarpal bone.

Image credit:
www.realbodywork.com

For this method, *we create a loop by connecting the thumb and the little finger of the same hand.* After the loop is established, we then try to prize them apart using the thumb and first finger of the other hand.

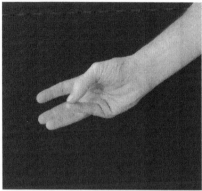

Right Hand (little finger and thumb joined)

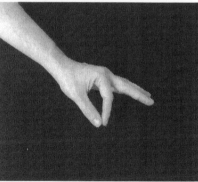

Left Hand (first finger and thumb joined)

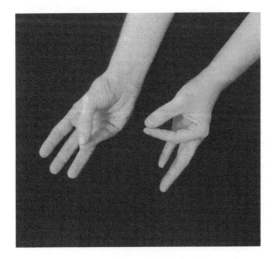

Left hand finger and thumb goes inside the loop made by right hand's little finger and thumb. Muscle test by trying to prize apart, with light to moderate pressure, the left hand's little finger and thumb using the right hand's finger and thumb.

The above picture is what it looks like when the muscle gives a "weak" or "unlocking" response. Meaning the loop made by the little finger and thumb of the right hand opens easily when pressure is applied.

The above picture is what it looks like when the muscles give a "strong" or "locked" response. In other words, the loop made by the little finger and thumb made by the right hand does not open easily when pressure is applied.

During any muscle testing, if the muscle responds as "strong" or "locked", this is an indicator that the body is saying "yes" because it is not stressed and therefore the muscle is able to operate at full capacity. However, if the muscle test responds as "weak" or "unlocked", this is an indicator that the body is saying "no" because it is in a stressed state and therefore the muscle is not able to work optimally. This is the fundamental principle of muscle testing and how we identify those things which support life force and those things that do not.

Let's try the following tests to gain a better understanding of this fundamental principle and to see it in action.

Smelling Test:
1. Smell a flower or some natural flower essences (without any additives) and then energy test yourself.
The smell of the flower is a natural, organic smell that supports life force so it should test up as 'strong' (yes).

2. Then try smelling a texta pen or some chemical then test again. What happens? Smelling the texta pen or chemical is an inorganic substance and therefore toxic to the body, so it will test up as 'weak' or 'no' response.

Yes and No Test:
1. Simply say, "Yes, yes, yes," repeatedly to yourself and self muscle test at the same time.

2. Now, say, "No, no, no," to yourself and self muscle test at the same time.

What did you discover?
If done correctly, saying, "Yes, yes, yes," will always test up as a strong (yes) response. Saying "No, no, no," will always test up as weak (no) response.

Image Test:
1. Create an image in the mind of a car crash, then self muscle test yourself.
2. Then create the image in the mind of a tree in an open field, then self muscle test yourself.

What happens?
The image of the car crash is an image of life being harmed or destroyed so the test should result as weak response (stress). The image of a tree is an image that supports life force so it should result as strong muscle response (yes).

Let's look at some images for testing.
1. Fix your gaze on the flower on the following page and muscle test yourself. Do you get a weak or strong response?

Image credit: Stan Shebs

2. Next, fix your gaze on this tank and muscle test yourself. Do you get a weak or strong response?

If done correctly and accurately, the flower will always test up as a strong response (supports life force). The tank will test up as a weak response (doesn't support life force).

Food Test:
1. Place a fruit or vegetable on your body or in your mouth and then self muscle test.
2. Then try placing a sugar candy or some processed food on your body or in your mouth and self muscle test again.

What did you discover?
If you place a fruit or vegetable on the body, 99% of the time the muscle will test up as strong (yes). If you place processed sugar on the body, the muscle will easily unlock and result as a weak muscle or a 'no' (stress) response.

Do you get the drift? You can use the list I provided at the beginning of the book to experiment. General rule of thumb— anything that is of the natural world that is unaltered by man, including any images of life like a flower, the sunrise, a field, mountains, etc., will test up as strong when you look at it or bring it into your energy field or eat it, etc. Anything that is toxic, poisonous, has harmful chemicals or holds images of destruction, war or violence will test up as weak because it causes your biological system stress.

So practice this until it becomes clearer and clearer for you. Again, always make sure you are switched on beforehand. Over time, you will gain more sensitivity and it will become easier to test. And over time also, you will become so sensitive to this reaction of the body's energies that you will feel it intuitively, you will feel the body shift and change its energetic structure quite often. We all have this ability and capacity already, yet we don't know how to sense it anymore. This muscle testing technique puts us back into contact with it.

Here is a list of other energy testing methods if the loop and finger method doesn't work for you:

- Using a hand held muscle testing device like the Tru-Tester. This is highly recommended for people who find self muscle testing difficult. The owner of the Tru-Tester calls this technique Applied Self Kinesiology, which is the same as self muscle testing. (www.trutester.com)

- Standing sway test - stand up in a relaxed fashion. For the strong response, most people will sway forwards, while for the weak response (stress), they will sway backwards.

- Let one finger be the one you will use for testing, and let another, on the same hand, the one you're testing with. So, extend the fingers on one hand, hold in mind the question or place the object on the body, then test by pushing down on one finger by using another finger on the same hand. Some people press on the middle finger with the index finger but, for me, I find it easier to press with the middle finger on the index finger. Take a look at the picture below.

- The sticky-smooth technique. Using any convenient smooth surface (credit cards are an option,, but it's better to have something without the magnetic strip), let one finger rub gently across the smooth surface. A smooth response indicates a yes and a rough, sticky response would indicate a stress or no response.

- A pendulum. Many people go with using a pendulum. It does work, but the problem with it is that most people who use it are "switched off" when working with it and, therefore, it gives misleading information. You can use it quite accurately if you are switched on and the question is for the highest good.

- Some people see different colors in their heads for strong and weak responses. Other people hear different sorts of sounds. The mind can easily play tricks with this one so I would advise to work with the other methods initially.

- On a subtle level, there is an energetic shift with anything that is held in mind. It can be experienced as subtle sensations within the body but one of the best ways to sense this shift is to hold your question or the image in mind and move your awareness to your heart center. Does the heart energy flow easily or does it feel tight and restricted? If it is flowing then it's a 'yes', so best to follow it, but if the heart space feels tight and restricted then it's a 'no', so best to avoid.

There are many ways to test, as you can see. I encourage you to experiment with a variety of them to work out which one feels better for you. I generally steer away from any testing method that requires me to have an instrument or some kind of material to be able to test. I don't want to be tied down to having an external object that I need to carry around with me everywhere. You have the capacity to test without instruments by simply using your body and mind.

If you are having troubles with it, that's quite normal; it takes time. If you really keen to delve deeper into this, I would encourage you to enroll onto an applied kinesiology course like "Touch for Health" so that you can learn from a teacher and in a group dynamic where you can practice this skill on others. In the course you will learn a clinical applied kinesiology method, and that's fine. Once you get the feeling of a weak and strong muscle, then you can really get more into the self testing techniques afterwards and feel more confident with them.

Testing Without Bias

To get accurate results, there needs to be no bias involved or invested interests in the outcome. This is one of the biggest obstacles with following any technique or spiritual path. There tends to be some self-interest involved, some attachment to some particular desire or outcome to be involved, and this is true in the self muscle testing process. If there is a desire for something to be a certain way when testing, then it's likely that it will give you uncertain and unclear answers.

The only way I have found to overcome any bias is to first 'check yourself'—if you sense bias then step back from yourself to gain a bigger picture and then drop it. Have a little moment to really take a look at the bigger picture to see if you're testing for selfish reasons. Often when you step back for a moment and check yourself, you can easily become detached when you can see a bigger picture and pull yourself out of your own little world for a moment. If you can do that, then it's likely that the energy test will be clear and accurate for that question.

Sometimes though, you just can't free yourself from the fact that there is some bias involved in your question and, deep down, you know it to be so. In such a case, it will be unlikely that you will receive a clear and correct answer and, therefore, it is simply best not to test and move on, or, if you know of someone who can do accurate muscle testing, then get him or her to test the question for you instead.

It is because of this tendency towards bias that I have found it much easier to test for other people or to test things that I have to no previous knowledge of. If you practice testing for other people or practice testing on things that you are not involved in, then you will get that 'feeling' of what it feels like to test when not attached to any particular outcome. After some time, you will get to know that 'feeling' of having no invested interest in an outcome, then you will easily be able to identify in yourself if you are testing with bias or not.

How to Ask a Question

There are only two responses or answers you can receive from a muscle test. You can only gain a 'yes' (this is good for my energy field) or a 'no' (this is a stress to my energy field) response from the muscle testing. The true art, therefore, comes from being able to ask the right and most relevant questions.

It also is a helpful and a recommended practice to incorporate "in the highest good" into your questioning. This brings in a higher level of intention and re-contextualizes the questioning so that all beings are considered and benefited by the results. Remember that all beings includes you, so you will also benefit from the results.

Try to be clear, precise and direct with your questioning. Be sure to have the question clear in your mind or write it down before testing. If you wait too long or ask a long-winded, confusing question, the results won't be clear and you may switch off in that time. Again, the art is in the ability to ask the right and most relevant questions.

Some examples of questions:

1. In the highest good, is this a wise purchase?

2. In the highest good, is it good for me to yoga class today at 6pm?

3. In the highest good, is this jam spread suitable to eat right now?

4. In the highest good, is it wise to call my friend … now?

5. In the highest good, is it good for me to go to this talk this afternoon?

6. In the highest good, is it wise for me to read this book?

7. In the highest good, is it good for me to apply for this job?

8. In the highest good, does this person need to eat more tomatoes?

9. In the highest good, is this vitamin required for my body right now? (Look at the vitamin bottle or place the vitamin on your body and then test, if no, move onto the next vitamin and so on. I will go into how to test for supplements in more detail later in this book.)

That's It!
So to summarize:
1. You need to be switched on to begin any testing and check yourself for any bias for what you are about to test. If you sense bias, step back from yourself and drop it.

2. Formulate and begin asking your questions. Add "for the highest good" to raise the level of intention. Conduct the self muscle test for one item or question at a time.

3. With the information received, you can now make a more informed decision.

The more tuned, balanced and calm your energy field is the more accurate responses you will receive. You have to develop the approach of a scientist, testing things without bias. Generally, I have found that most people who are interested in this stuff, are willing to experiment with it, practice it and pursue it further, will get about 70%-80% accuracy.

Exploring the World with Self Muscle Testing

The following chapters of this book are dedicated to how you can apply self muscle testing in daily life. The following are just examples of how you can use it and it is in no way limited to using it in relation to these areas. Once you get more and more familiar with muscle testing and the subtleties of how energy feels when it is switched on or off, please feel free to explore in all areas of your life.

Testing Health Products and Supplements

Using the muscle test for testing health products is one of the best uses I have found. I personally think all health food shops should have a qualified applied kinesiologist available in store to help people identify which supplements and foods would be most suitable for them. We are continuously bombarded by health product advertising, all claiming the next big super food, and I have found that most of it is false, a waste of time and money and only serves to confuse people about their health.

We don't need to read 10,000 books on different theories of dieting or do a PhD on nutrition to find out which foods and products work for us. The body already knows what it requires to regain health and balance; we have just lost the connection and the ability to hear this truth inside us. Muscle testing provides us with a way to bypass the ego mind and reconnect to our body's innate intelligence. Therefore, being able to do the self muscle test can reduce all the unnecessary spending, over analyzing and excess spending when selecting health products or identifying nutritional requirements for healing.

I have found that, often, it is just one or two herbs or vitamins that a person needs a boost of at any one particular time that acts to rebalance the whole system.

So, when you go to the supermarket or the chemist store, you can use energy testing to uncover <u>exactly</u> what supplement or health product that your body requires for health and healing.

This is how to do it:
1. Switch on. Check that you are feeling switched on and without bias to an outcome.

2. You can look directly at or place the product or supplement bottle on the body and say something like, "The vitamin/product my body needs most to heal is this," or "This is the vitamin required for my body right now?" Test.

3. If it tests as weak, your body doesn't agree or require that particular product.

4. Next vitamin. Repeat Step 2.

5. When it tests strong, it's a "yes". Grab it and put it to the side.

6. Continue this process for a while and put to the side any products that have tested up as 'yes'.

7. After a while, you can ask, "This is all that I require at this time?"
If it tests strong, it's a "yes" so you don't have to continue anymore. If it tests weak, you can say something like, "There is another vitamin or product that my body needs that is here?" or something along those lines. Test—if it comes back as 'yes', keep testing. If it comes back as 'no' then there is no other product you require right now. Move to step 8 if you have a few different products that initially tested up as 'yes'.

8. So, you may have a handful of vitamins or products that you have collected. Now we can narrow it down. Look at the first one and say something like, "Is this vitamin the highest priority for my body to heal?"—test. If it is a 'yes', put it to the side again. If it is a 'no', put it back on the shelf.

9. You will eventually narrow it down to 1-3 items. These are the best for you at this time.

Dosages

When it comes to how much to take and how often to take it, I have found the labels are inaccurate (too small doses). Most of the time they are regulated by the Governing bodies which usually under prescribe vitamins and minerals because they either have no idea of the benefits and want to play it safe, or maybe they are afraid that if people took larger doses it may provide great healing results and therefore threaten the pharmaceutical industry. Of course, be sensible with this, even vitamins and natural supplements can be toxic in excess.

If you are unsure about your testing skills, it's best to see a kinesiologist or nutritionally orientated physician who could give you more accurate information. But know that you can use energy testing to get gain more correct information relating to your body and current needs in relation to medicine, herbs, foods and supplements.

I am an advocate of mega dose vitamin therapy but this is a controversial subject in medicine, one that requires you to do your own research or speak to a suitable health professional who has extensive training in nutrition. Most of the recommended doses on vitamin bottles are very conservative amounts and unlikely to have any effect. Another issue worth mentioning here is that many of the manufacturing of vitamins and mineral supplements are coming into question mainly regarding the quality of the products.

Therefore, best to take only high quality supplements from reputable companies. If you would like to know more about mega dose vitamin therapy, then please read books, such as: *Doctor Yourself* by Andrew Saul, *Orthomolecular Treatment for Schizophrenia* or *How to Live Longer and Feel Better* by Linus Pauling, before committing to larger doses of vitamins.

It is possible, however, to use muscle testing to help you with the dosages. (Please speak with your nutritionally orientated physician if you are unsure or before taking larger than normal doses.)

To test for dosages:
1. Look at the item and say something like, "How many tablets do I take, 1?" Test. "Two?" Test. "Three?" Test, and so on, until you get a strong indicator meaning "Yes".

2. "How many times per day? Twice a day?" Test. "Three times a day?" Test. "Four times a day?" Test, and so on.

3. "How long for? One week?" Test. "Two Weeks?" Test, and so on.

After this process, you will have all the information you need regarding that particular supplement including which one to take, how many tablets to take at one time, how many times a day and how long to take it for. Done. Stick to what it has indicated and see what happens. It's natural to have a few doubts and be cautious about this at first. Over time, as you get more confident and see the results of this, it's likely that it there will be little to no doubt about the effectiveness of this process.

Feel free to experiment with it. Use the muscle test on essential oils, flower essences, crystals, incense, foods, minerals, vitamins, herbal mixtures and so on.

Testing Foods

Testing appropriate foods is easy but, to receive accurate testing, be sure not to carry bias regarding certain foods as this will surely interfere with the testing. This is often hard to achieve as we are bombarded daily regarding what is considered a healthy food and what it is not. What I have discovered is that, generally, what is presented and advertised as healthy foods is true, but in a lot of cases it is not.

There are a lot of factors that influence whether the food will be beneficial or stressful to our system. What is not often discussed or acknowledged is the current energetic state of a particular individual in any given moment. In one moment yogurt may be beneficial to their system, due to the right timing, the right chemistry in the body and the right ph. levels etc. However, in an hour's time, it may not be beneficial due to the changes in energetics, chemistry and so on.

Energetics are constantly changing; yin and yang are constantly moving into each other and influencing each other. Therefore, it could be said that no food is absolutely healthy and beneficial all of the time. One must learn to become sensitive to the energetic changes in our systems to correctly identify which foods at what times are suitable for that particular moment. And this is where muscle testing comes in. It can provide us an in-the-moment feedback system to which foods are beneficial or stressful to us now, in this very moment.

This is how you go about testing.

1. Make sure you're switched on and check yourself. Remove any bias.

2. Focus your gaze onto one of the foods you are considering. Keep your gaze on it.

3. The question, "This food is beneficial and healthy for me?"

4. Test. Strong response is a "yes", weak response is a "no".

5. If you receive a weak response, simply move your gaze over to another food item, repeat the question and test.

6. Continue this process until you discover the items that are suitable for you right now. From your test results, simply choose one or two from the beneficial list you have gathered.

7. Whilst eating and after eating, notice how the body feels when eating and how the body manages the digestion of these foods. In most cases, digestion will be easy. A sure sign that a particular food is stressful on the system is a sluggish or uneasy digestive process.

Testing People

Because muscle testing helps us to identify that which supports life and that which harms or causes stress, we can actually use it to test other people. This can be a handy skill when you are looking to employ people to work in your business, or when choosing a teacher to follow or when choosing someone to trust with something important.

People, just like any other object, calibrate at different levels of energy, either expressing energy in a supportive and uplifting manner or as an energy force that doesn't support life force. This can easily be explained as someone who takes more energy from others and objects than they give out. Those who support life force generally give more energy out than they take from the universe. Ideally, when choosing to work with people or get close to people we really need to consider what kind of energy they are emitting and choose only to work closely with those who support life force.

Through this process you may come to find some of your close friends and associates are actually harmful to your life force and this may prove confronting. It may be helpful to reflect on this and question why you tend to hang out with them and what is the actual relationship based on. When you question and reflect on your relationships in this way, things may become more obvious to you and, from that, correct action will arise. In many cases, it will become obvious that the friendship or relationship will need to discontinue. Do not be disheartened because, when we clear out negative or unsupportive energy fields from our lives, it makes space for more positive and supportive energy fields to come in. Eventually, from following this path there will be little—if any—negative or harmful energy fields within close vicinity and life will take on a new sense of buoyancy and enthusiasm.

To test people initially, it will help to have a picture of the particular person you wish to test. Ideally, the picture will be clear and contain no other individuals in the picture frame.

1. Switch yourself on, check yourself, clear bias.

2. Fix your gaze on the picture of the person.

3. Ask the question, "For the highest good, is this person supportive of life force?" or "For the highest good, does this person have a healthy life force?"

4. If the test is strong then, yes, they are good to have around. If it tests weak there is a strong chance they are not good to have around. Reflect on it for a bit and retest on another day. If the test comes back again as weak, then it's up to you what to do with that information.

Here are some pictures of people through history. Try muscle testing while looking at each photo.

1.

2.

3.  4.

What do you notice? What did you discover?

Only one person in this set of images will produce a "weak" muscle response. Which one is it?

Image 1 – Johann Sebastian Bach
Image 2 – Adolf Hitler Image credit Bundesarchiv, Bild 146-1990-048-29A / CC-BY-SA
Image 3 – Swami Vivekeananda
Image 4 – Gangaji Image credit Gangaji Foundation

Testing Purchases

Muscle testing can be used when shopping and making purchases and can therefore save us a lot of money by reducing unnecessary spending. Coming up with an appropriate question to help one decipher whether a particular purchase is a good choice or not was a little tricky at first. However, I have discovered that simply asking if it would be a wise purchase is often enough to establish whether the purchase would be beneficial or not.

1. Switch yourself on, check yourself, remove bias.

2. Fix your gaze on the object and ask the following question, "Is purchasing this item a wise decision?" or "Buying this item now is wise?"

3. Test.

4. If it tests as strong it would be a good purchase. If it tests up weak the purchase is not a good one, move on.

Testing for Health and Healing

When one gets ill or feels out of balance, a natural reaction is to seek help from a health professional or healer of some kind. There are 100s of different modalities available to us in the modern world and millions of different healers. Each modality offers a unique and specialized field of practice. I have come to discover that different modalities are required at different times in our lives as we grow and evolve. Therefore, one modality, let's say chiropractic, worked at one point in your life and addressed an illness but a few years later it doesn't seem to work for you like it used to. Therefore, it's probably time to open up to another modality.

It's the same with the healers or practitioners that you meet along the way. One practitioner may really help you out for a period but its likely that after a few years they won't be able to help you any longer and this is a sign that you need to open up to somebody else. Please note: In any case of serious health concerns please consult your medical doctor. In most cases complementary medicine works well alongside western medicine, therefore I recommend to use them alongside each other to help balance each other out.

When you are faced with a time when you are seeking healing, using self-muscle testing to identify which modality is most suitable can cut through any confusion you may have. I can also save you a lot of time and money exploring different modalities trying to find the one that works for you.

Some modalities are more traditional in the sense that you are 1-on -1 with a health practitioner. However, other modalities may include health programs or trainings in which the patient establishes a self practice by utilizing a variety of techniques, like yoga, for example.

When self muscle testing the following table, try first gazing at one box at a time and avoid looking at the individual words when testing. This helps when muscle testing a large amount of data, such as scanning charts or large tables of information. Ask a question like, "In the highest good, the modality that would best serve me at this time is in this box?"

When you identify the box, now break it down further by looking at the numbers on the left side of the words and in the case of the 3rd box giving a strong response, ask a question like, "In the highest good, the modality that would best serve me now is between 21 – 25?" If it tests as weak, change the question to: "In the highest good, the modality that would best serve me now is between 26 – 30?"

Once you have found which group the modality is in, break it down even further by asking a question like, "In the highest good, the modality that would best serve me now is 21? 22? 23?"

After you have done it this way, you would have identified one modality that would be best suited to you now.

Ok, so let's practice. On the following page is a list of healing modalities to get you started. Use a question similar to the examples given above ("In the highest good, the modality that would best serve me at this time is in this box?").

Table of Healing Modalities

BOX 1	BOX 3
1. Remedial massage	21. Acupressure
2. Swedish massage	22. Aromatherapy
3. Thai massage	23. Astrology
4. Chiropractic	24. Ayurvedic medicine
5. Physiotherapy	25. Auricular (ear) therapy
6. Osteopathy	26. Alexander Technique
7. Reiki	27. Biofeedback
8. Theta healing	28. Bach Flowers remedies
9. Crystal healing	29. Crystal therapy
10. Acupuncture (Chinese medicine)	30. Naturopathy
BOX 2	**BOX 4**
11. Acupuncture (dry needling)	31. Hot Yoga
12. Hypnosis	32. Gentle Yoga
13. Counseling	33. Feldenkrais
14. Psychology	34. Pilates
15. Emotional Freedom Technique (EFT)	35. Tai Chi
16. Sound healing	36. Qi Gong
17. Music therapy	37. Kung Fu
18. Art therapy	38. Karate
19. Applied Kinesiology	39. Tae Kwon Do
20. Neural Organizing Technique	40. Capoiera

More Advanced Techniques

Scales from 1-10

You can use a scale from 1-10 to gain more detail and to compare various things in relation to each other and the highest good. For example, you may have a few supplements that you have already tested and they both came back as a 'yes' response. So you can use the scale from 1-10 to uncover which one holds the highest 'yes' or truth for you in that moment.

You can use the 1-10 scale like this:
1. Switch yourself on, check yourself, clear bias.

2. First, do the general energy test that we have already discussed in this book to work out a "yes" or "no" response from a variety of supplements. When you have a few 'yes' items in front of you we can use the scale from 1-10.

3. The question is something like, "From 1-10, 10 being the highest good and 1 being the lowest, this product (look at, or place on body) is between 1-5?" Test.

4. If given a weak response, next question is, "From 1-10, 10 being the highest good and 1 being the lowest, this product (look at, or place on body) is between 6-10?" Test.

5. Whatever one indicated as strong (yes), then break it down into smaller bits. It is 6? Test. It is 7? Test. It is 8? Test. And so on, until you get the number.

6. Then repeat the process for the other supplement you are testing.

7. At the end of testing the items, you will know which one is of the highest priority, so go with that.

I find using the scale from 1-10 helps me to identify which options or choices hold the highest truth. Often, I will use it when I have multiple options available to me, like which course to study or what job to pursue. I simply write down all the options on a piece of paper and then go through each one and get it on the scale of 1-10, including "for the highest good" in the questioning. This process really helps me to clarify which option will be of the highest service to myself and to others. For the example below, I list 5 different courses that I am interested in studying.

1. I first write down all of my options, including the name of the course and the year I would start the course. I would also include things like "full-time" or "part-time" to gain more clarification.

2. I switch myself on and check myself that I feel switched on and clear any bias.

3. I would look at the piece of paper where I have written the course and say something like, "For the highest good, on a scale from 1-10, 10 being the highest and 1 being the lowest, studying a Bachelor in Acupuncture in 2013 is between 1-5?" Test.

4. If received a weak response I would ask again, 6-10. "For the highest good, on a scale from 1-10, 10 being the highest and 1 being the lowest, studying a Bachelor in Acupuncture in 2013 is between 6-10?" Test.

5. Then, depending on which one came back as 'yes', I would then break it down into smaller parts. It is 6? Test. It is 7? Test. It is 8? Test. And so on. Once the exact number is identified, I would write it down next to the course and then move on to testing the next course option.

6. I would repeat the process for all the 5 items on my list to get the full picture.

7. Then, based on that information, I would make my decision.

Non-Local Advanced Testing Method

The most common method, and the one explored within this book, is to seek answers from within the framework of one's own body or mind and therefore may be referred to as "local muscle testing". The other, more abstract and mind blowing, method is the ability to seek answers from the greater field of consciousness itself which is not limited to one's own mind and body.

The field of consciousness is a field of information and energy that exists within us, all around us, and throughout the entire universe. We all have the capacity to directly communicate with this field of consciousness and the muscle testing process is one method in which to do it. The muscle testing method allows us to ask 'yes' and 'no' questions to the field of consciousness, and this has the potential to rapidly open up our understanding of the universe. This method of testing is referred to as non-local muscle testing.

To learn more about this, I would recommend reading *Power vs. Force* by Dr. David Hawkins to get a real thorough explanation of this phenomenon.

Conclusion

If you have made it to the end of this book you will now have a good understanding of a variety of practical exercises that you can do in regards to the self muscle testing method.

In summary:
1. Harbor a lifestyle that allows your energy and nervous system to be "switched on" more then switched off. Surround yourself with those things which support life (natural beauty, uplifting people etc.) and endeavor to live a moral life. Avoid those things that don't support life.

2. When testing make sure you're switched on, utilizing one or more of the techniques explained in the book.

3. Check yourself for bias; clear it out (no expectation, no preconceived beliefs).

4. Gaze gently at the object in question or place it on your body.

5. Use a clear and direct yes or no question. Add "In the highest good" to give it more power.

6. Test using the muscle in the hand or via one of the other methods explored in this book.

7. Continue to question if scanning objects or using the number scale. When you receive your "yes" response, take note and go with it. Trust it.

I recommend that you experiment with this testing method to help you to fine tune your intuition and to help develop your energetic sensitivity. Be sure to be active in 'switching on' and, if it makes sense to you, make the effort and commitment to align your lifestyle with only those things that will support your energy field. By elevating your own energy field you will naturally and automatically uplift and inspire those around you.

Know that we all have the full and complete truth of things already inside of us waiting to be rediscovered. We only need to work at quieting the mental noise in order to hear this deeper truth more fully, and the self muscle testing method is one tool that will help us do this.

~ May all Beings be Happy ~

Other Books by the Author

Chakra Balancing Made Simple and Easy

Meditation Made Simple

How to Do Restorative Yoga

Autumn Oriental Yoga

The Little Book of Yin

How to Learn Acupuncture

Simply Zen Quotes

98900463R00047

Made in the USA
Middletown, DE
10 November 2018